Are You Squared Away?
First Edition – Binocular View

Published by Objectively Authentic
Publishing

ISB 979-8-218-45976-5

9 798218 459765

Are You Squared Away?

By:

Kalvin R. Johnson

Dedication & Thank-You

I give thanks to God, the Almighty, for bringing everything together. I dedicate this book to my mother, Cheri R. Johnson. I miss you so much. It has been 10 years since you left us, but I still know you are with me. I miss you, Momma! Thank you, Dad, for constantly trying to make things better. If it weren't for you, I wouldn't have the mentality to compete and win. I believe that my parents did their best. Thank you to my siblings for being who you are in life. I will always be there for my family and friends, no matter what! As a result, I am aware of the concept of responsibility and expectation. To every one of the shoulders that I have stood on and will continue to stand on, so that I can support others to their greatness. Thank you to those who helped me along the way. A special thanks to everyone for all the dedication. Thank you for believing in OA. All the blood, sweat, and tears paid off.

It is my daughter to whom I also dedicate this book. My desire was for both of us to have a book. Thanks for providing the motivation. Ever since you were born, you have helped me become a better person. You are always the force that drives me the most. This is for you!

As I wrote this, I received news of my childhood friend being murdered in the streets of Virginia. Rest in Peace, Bradley K. Kortbawi. Gateway for life. His life was taken because of racial prejudice. Let this book help people see a different perspective on how to love and maneuver.

Preface

God is energy. Life is full of energy and emotion (energy in motion). Knowing that energy exists is a great knowledge for a person to understand how energy is passed or maybe, how God works. Being as objective as possible before action has proved to be more successful, and we do not need statistics to know that. For what it is worth, I wrote this book with a broad stroke for all people to read, regardless of religion or social status.

One definition of objectivity is the absence of bias or prejudice in the presentation of facts. Associations, socialization, opinions, cultural trends, and natural selection all coexist in the environment we inhabit. Aesthetics refers to the study of or the practice of appreciating beauty. Subjective beauty is the antithesis of objective beauty since it is based on or influenced by the observer's own subjective emotions, preferences, and judgments. Sounding like an oxymoron, "Objectively Aesthetic" or "OA" is a useful introduction to common experience. There is a great deal of prejudice in one's own subjective experience. In a crazy, biased world, OA strives to present a varied and impartial perspective to impact decision-making and behavior.

As the creator of OA, with 20 years of service in the United States Air Force, I retired at the rank of Master Sergeant. As an Industrial and Organizational (I/O) scholar and practitioner, I am passionate about fostering the growth and success of individuals and organizations worldwide. While single-handedly raising my now-adult daughter, I faced personal challenges that shaped my perspective. These unique experiences, combined with my own journey of growth and development, taught me that things are not always what they seem at first glance.

I look forward to many editions to the wonderful journey God has sent me on.

Introduction

SALT is a comprehensive framework that integrates Light and Love into every aspect of life, offering guidance in spiritual growth, empathy, leadership, and relational dynamics, allowing individuals to navigate life with clarity, purpose, and fulfillment by embodying Reverence, Intentionality, Objectivity, and Togetherness.:

Squared Away Light Theory focuses on spiritual growth and empathy, promoting Reverence through connecting with higher principles and fostering Authentic Empathy for genuine connections. Liberating Leadership encourages Objectivity by empowering autonomy and collaboration, achieving collective success through Enlightened Togetherness.

Squared Away Life Theory guides purpose-driven living by Observing Reverence in active engagement, Orienting with Intentionality to align actions with values, Deciding with Objectivity for meaningful choices, and acting with purpose towards personal and collective growth.

Squared Away Leadership Theory equips leaders with Reverence-based structural integrity, fosters Intentionality through Human Resources development, applies Objectivity in navigating organizational dynamics, and inspires Togetherness with symbolic Leadership.

Squared Away Love Theory (Enlightened Togetherness) explores love's dynamics: Reverence as its foundation, Intentionality in friendships, Objectivity in partnerships for resilience, and Togetherness in relationships, nurturing emotional bonds.

SALT provides a holistic framework for navigating life's challenges with clarity, purpose, and fulfillment, integrating Reverence, Intentionality, Objectivity, and Togetherness across spiritual, personal, professional, and relational dimensions for meaningful living and leadership.

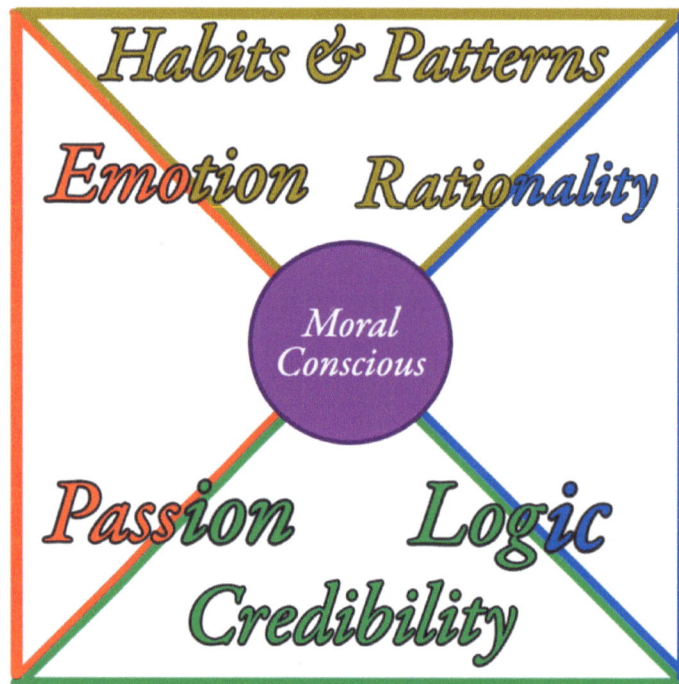

Light

Love

Life

Leadership

Habits & Patterns

Emotion

Rationality

Moral Conscious

Passion

Logic

Credibility

Squared
Away Light

Spiritual Transcendence (Light)

Spiritual Transcendence encourages individuals to practice Light energy pursue a greater purpose and connect with the spiritual realm. Get to know yourself and connect with a higher power or consciousness to find purpose beyond of this world. This requires transcending ego, material desires, and **understanding** Quantum Physics. This kind of **understanding** may provide genuine purpose and fulfillment beyond basic requirements. Practicing **Reverence** (Love) leads to having deep respect for a higher purpose and leading to Enlightenment (Light), the highest form of love.

Authentic Empathy (Life)

This framework emphasizes having **Intentionality** by prioritizing genuine empathy. This method shows how important it is to connect with others genuinely, without judging them or having any secret goals. Active listening, truly trying to **understand** other people's points of view, and being kind without any secret goals are all important. This method not only makes links between people stronger, but it also improves mental health, which leads to deeper longer-lasting interactions. Willingness stresses having Intentionality by putting real concern first.

Liberating Leadership (Lead)

This framework focuses on **Objectivity** by fostering autonomy, trust, and collaboration. Objectiveness is at the heart of this system, which encourages independence, trust, and unity. Value each person's unique skills and points of view and push them to reach their full potential. This method gives people power and encourages them instead of controlling or stifling them, making a space where everyone can do well. Objectively examine Intentionality.

Enlightened Togetherness (Love)

This framework is the idea of **Togetherness**. To be together, you need to put teamwork, unity, and a common goal at the top of your list. Real progress and success happens when people work together without fighting, whether they are working alone or with groups. People and groups can get more done and feel more united and successful when they work together with similar values and goals. Use Reverence, Intentionality, Objectivity and TOGETHERNESS!

4 Ways to
Spiritual Transcendence
[Reverence]

Connection with Higher Consciousness (Enlightenment)

Explore the idea of a world beyond the material world and try to connect with a higher power or awareness to reach a higher level of spirituality. Some examples are prayer and traditions, meditative practices, community and friendship, and awareness. There is a bigger picture! Having deep respect for life should bring peace.

Inner Self Exploration (Peace)

Deep self-reflection, studying your inner thoughts and feelings to learn more about yourself and find a higher purpose, can help you reach spiritual transformation. Some examples are therapy (like counseling or mindfulness-based methods), vacations and time alone, and making art. Finding joy to spread.

Transcending Ego and Material Desires (Joy)

Achieve spiritual transcendence by actively trying to go beyond the ego and material wants. This will help you understand your purpose in a deeper way that goes beyond your basic needs. Some examples are getting rid of unnecessary things in your life and becoming less attached to material things; focused on your what is needed instead of wanted. Do not be distracted!

Purposeful Living (Love)

Acknowledge spirituality by ensuring your actions are in line with a higher purpose and focusing on living a life that goes beyond your basic wants and needs and leads to more spiritual satisfaction. Aligning your life and vocation goals with a higher purpose is one example. So are careful eating and health, and so is finding ways to make a real difference in other people's lives. This leads to Authentic Empathy.

4 Ways to
Authentic Empathy
[Intentionality]

Genuine Understanding (Observe)

Genuinely show empathy by trying to see things from someone else's point of view and recognizing their feelings and experiences without forcing your own. Actively listening to others without talking over them or giving answers right away are two examples. Another is validating others' feelings without passing judgment.

Active Listening (Orient)

Show genuine care by listening to others without talking over them or judging what they have to say. This will help them feel truly heard. Some examples are repeating what someone said to make sure you understood, asking open-ended questions, and showing agreement without words by making eye contact and nodding.

Kindness Without Explanation (Decide)

Show real understanding by being kind and joy to others without expecting anything in return. This will help you want to help others without having any secret goals or other reasons. Being there for others without expecting anything in return, doing random acts of kindness for strangers, and finding a way to make someone's day a little better without expecting anything in return are all examples of this.

Deep Connection Building (Act)

Building through empathy is crucial in this phase, fostering trust, responsiveness, and adaptability. Empathy helps in implementing decisions, resolving conflicts, and strengthening relationships. By incorporating empathy into actions, individuals achieve objectives, foster deeper connections, and improve outcomes and relationships. This leads to Liberating Leadership.

4 Ways to Liberating Leadership
[Objectivity]

Squared Away Light Theory

Collaborative Environment (Structure)

Set up an environment where working together is not only welcomed but also respected. Stress the value of working together and encourage a culture where different skills & points of view are valued and used for the team's benefit. Some examples are encouraging conversation that includes everyone, showing thanks and praise, & working together across departments with different skills and points of view.

Individual Growth and Development (Human Resources)

Value each person's skills and ideas and help them grow as a person and in their career. Give them chances to learn new things and improve the ones they already have. Recognize and support their unique skills to help them reach their full potential. Different kinds of learning chances, reviews and praise, and individual growth goals are some examples.

Empowerment Through Autonomy (Political)

Help people make choices and take responsibility for their work. Help and direct when needed, but let people choose how to complete jobs on their own, which will build a sense of responsibility and freedom. Clear goal making, frequent check-ins and feedback, and training and skill development are some examples.

Trust-Based Relationships (Symbolic)

Start building trust by showing that you believe in your team's skills. When you trust their knowledge and judgment, they are more likely to take chances, come up with new ideas, and bring their own unique views to the table. Some examples are confidently giving away responsibilities, recognizing and appreciating contributions, and encouraging new ideas and taking risks. This leads to Enlightened Togetherness!

4 Ways to
Enlightened Togetherness
[Love]

Alignment of Shared Values (Human)

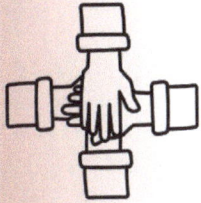

Show awareness of togetherness by making sure that people or groups share the same beliefs. This will create an environment where everyone works together to reach the same goals. Setting common principles and a purpose, supporting diversity and inclusion, and working together to set goals and make plans are some examples.

Collective Goal Setting (Friendship)

Getting everyone involved in setting and describing group goals. This will help people feel like they have a common cause and are committed to reaching those goals. Collaborative talks, in which everyone helps set goals for the group, and training on joint vision and purpose are two examples.

Open Communication Channels (Partnership)

Encouraging open and honest conversation. This will create an environment where people can easily share their thoughts and points of view, which will help them work together better. Open communication tools, active listening and polite comments, and making decisions together are some examples.

Recognition of Individual Contributions (Love)

Recognizing and appreciating the unique things that each person brings to the group. Create a culture that values the skills and strengths that each person brings to the group effort. Some examples are working together based on strengths, making decisions with everyone in mind, and showing respect and praise. Understanding (Reason) leads to Overstanding (Love). Squared Away (Light) Theory transcends to Life.

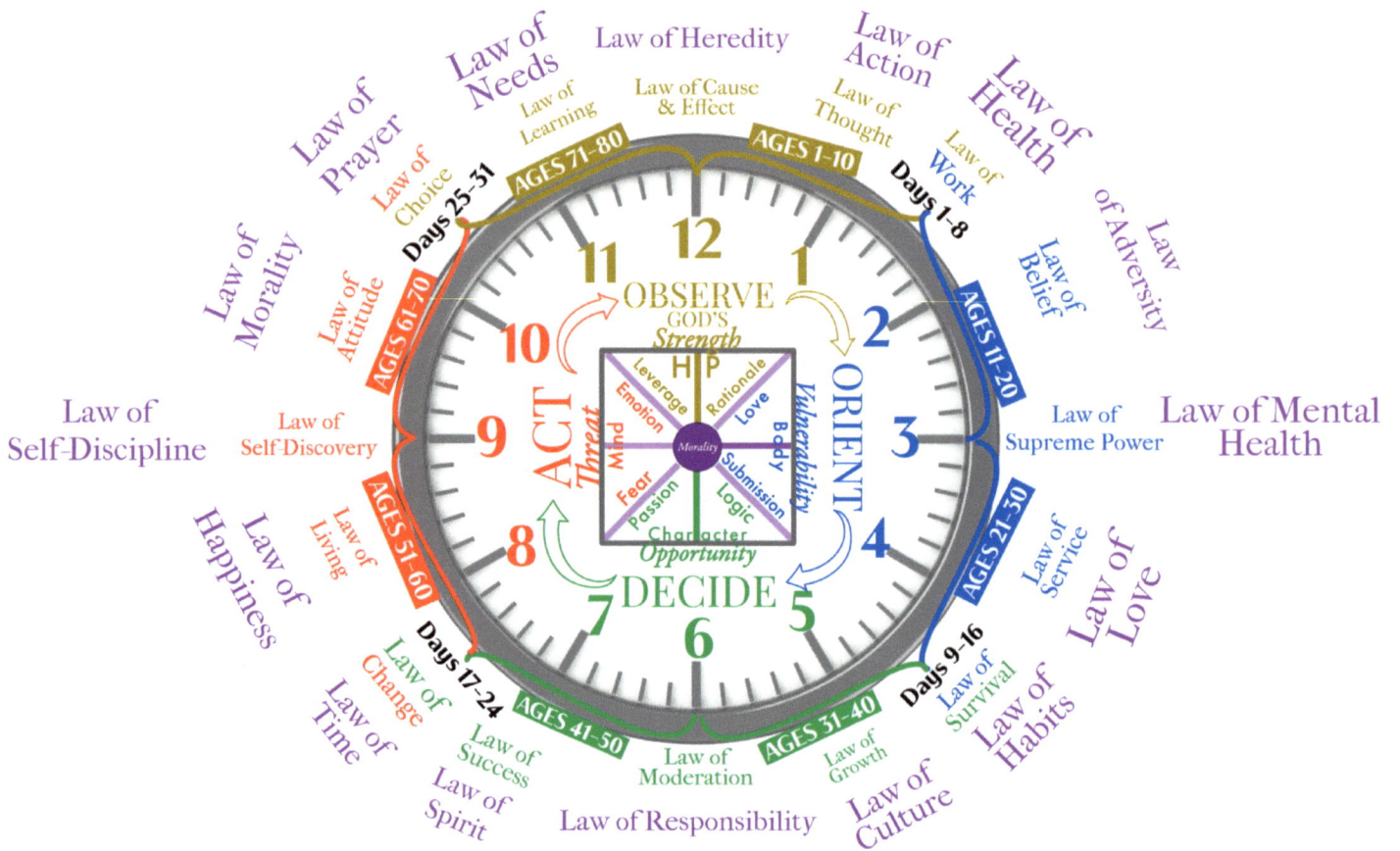

Squared Away Life Theory

Observe

Reverence is the predominant emotional state for LOVE. The practice asks us to interact with the world not as silent viewers but as active players in the story of life that is always going on. Being more amazed, deeply respectful, and responsible for the world and everything in it is what it pushes us to do.

Orient

Intentionality encourages that we think about our values, beliefs, and personal experiences within this context. People are encouraged to look into their pasts and stories to see how they affect how they see the world. By consciously positioning ourselves in this way, we can make sure that our actions are more in line with who we really are. This will give our lives more meaning and character.

Decide

To make a more important life path, making choices that are in line with observations and values is what it means to decide with **Objectivity**. Choosing ways that are in line with your values and show that you have a deep understanding of your direction is an important part of meaningful life guidance.

Act

To be together, people should put meaningful action based on their observations, beliefs, and choices at the top of their list of priorities. People are told to do something about their goals instead of just talking about problems. People can grow and feel fulfilled by putting their values and goals into action. This can also help them feel like they are working toward the same goals as others. **Togetherness**.

4 Ways to Observe
[Reverence]

Environmental Stewardship

Take an active role in taking care of the world. Adopt eco-friendly habits and help protect the environment. Some examples are recycling, being an aware shopper, conservation efforts, saving energy, and saving water. Being intentional in all aspects of life is a choice.

Mindful Presence

Show reverence by being mindfully present, focusing on the current moment, and understanding how everything is linked. This will help you appreciate the story of life more. Mindful breathing, observing nature, and incorporating awareness into daily life are all examples of ways to practice mindfulness.

Cultural Respect

Show reverence by recognizing and valuing the importance of different cultures, customs, and histories and by helping to keep them alive and help people understand them. Educating and raising knowledge about different cultures and encouraging acceptance and respect for everyone. Being unbiased and objective.

Active Contribution

Whether it's through creation, community service, or making moral choices, active participation changes the story of existence and lives up to the ideals of reverence. Community participation, responsible decision-making, thoughtful living, and artistic expression with reverence are a few examples. This should lead to a better orientation of Life.

4 Ways to Orient
[Intentionality]

**Squared Away
Life Theory**

Purposeful Exploration

Take the time to think about your situations and beliefs. Try to figure out how they affect your choices and behaviors. This intentional journey helps you get in touch with your true self and life's meaning. Some examples are doing activities to clarify your ideals, becoming more self-aware, and thinking to find trends.

Authentic Alignment

Try to make sure that your behaviors are in line with who you really are. Connect your ideals and views with the things you do every day by using purposeful direction. A better feeling of purpose and authenticity grows from this connection. Setting short- & long-term true goals that are in line with your ideals and making daily practices are two examples.

Narrative Awareness

Know that your past and personal story influence how you see the world. Figure out how these things affect how people see things. Being aware of this lets you connect with your true self more consciously. Self-reflection and writing in a diary are two examples. So are culture study and experience and careful listening.

Reflective Practice

Take the time to think about your own thoughts and experiences. Regularly thinking about yourself can help you see and understand the things that shape your view of the world. This leads to a life that is aligned with meaning and authenticity. Mindfulness meditation is a way to think critically about your beliefs and test them.

4 Ways to Decide
[Objectivity]

Value-Based Choices

Use facts and findings to help you make choices. Use these ideas to help you make decisions that are in line with your ideals and what you see in the world. Decisions based on facts, critical thought and study, and principles harmony and reflection are some examples.

Align with Observations

Base decisions on observations and factual information. Use these insights to guide choices toward paths that resonate with your values and observations of the world. Examples include data-driven decision-making; critical thinking and research; & values alignment and reflection.

Reflective Decision-Making

When making choices, think about what you've seen and what you believe in. Think about how the choices you make fit with your beliefs and help you move forward in a useful way. Some examples are meditating or other forms of contemplation to clear your mind and talking to teachers or trusted experts to learn more about how your choices align with your values.

Meaningful Life Direction

Make choices that will help you live a worthwhile life. When making decisions, being objective means picking roads that lead to a meaningful life. Think about how each choice fits into the bigger story of your life. Identifying your core beliefs and life purpose, thinking about the effects on the future, and being open to learning and growing are some examples.

4 Ways to Act
[Togetherness]

Squared Away Life Theory

Purposeful Action

Focus on why you are doing what you are doing. Make sure that each step is based on what you've seen, what you know, & what you've decided. Purposeful action fosters togetherness by coordinating individual efforts with common objectives. Setting clear goals & objectives that are in line with your purpose is one example. Another is working with others to make sure that everyone's efforts are directed toward the same goal.

Manifest Values

Action is the best way to make your ideals and goals come true. Instead of just talking about problems, let your deeds show what you believe, which will help you grow and be happy. Including principles in daily life, helping and getting involved in the community, and setting and working toward personal goals are all examples.

Foster Personal Growth

Do things that help you grow and feel fulfilled as a person. Let your actions be driven by a sense of purpose and in line with what you've learned and what you've decided, so they help you grow. As examples, we can use ongoing learning and skill growth, as well as thoughtful routines and critical thinking.

Create Togetherness

Create a feeling of togetherness through your actions. Showing shared values and goals through your deeds will help people work together and feel like they are part of a group. Community work projects, team-building events, and putting together shared efforts are some examples.

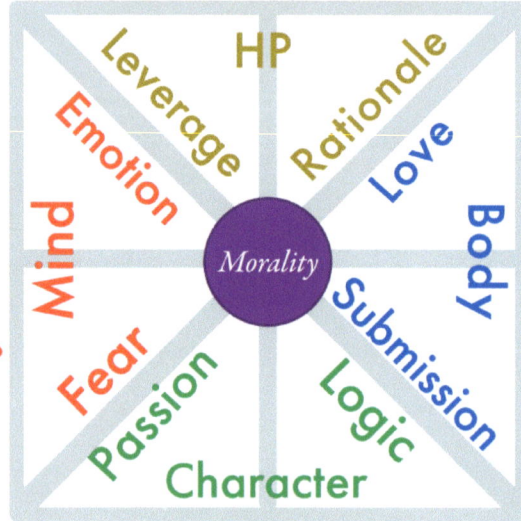

Freeze
(New Beginning)

DISCOVERY & PLAN
Observe Strengths
Structural

Unfreeze
(Let Go)

Symbolic · *Manage Threats*

DESTINY & ACT

Orient w/ Vulnerability · **Human Resources**

DREAM & DO

HP
Leverage
Emotion
Rationale
Love
Mind
Body
Morality
Submission
Fear
Passion
Logic
Character

Political
Decide on Opportunities

DESIGN & STUDY

Change
(Neutral Zone)

Change
(Neutral Zone)

Squared Away Leadership Theory

Structural (Observe)

Reverence by placing an emphasis on the organization's formal structure, hierarchies, responsibilities, and procedures, this framework aims to foster Reverence. Aligning the structure of the organization with its broad aims, improving processes for efficiency, and ensuring job functions are clear are all part of this. The most important thing is to take this framework seriously and value the order and stability it aims to provide to the business.

Human Resources (Orient)

Intentionality is a key component of this concept, which states that leaders should prioritize the growth and happiness of their people. To succeed in the long run, they need to realize that people are the most important asset any company has and that investing in a talented and enthusiastic staff is a requirement. To accomplish corporate objectives in an efficient manner, this method places an emphasis on cooperation, employee empowerment, and personal development.

Political (Decide)

Objectivity. A leader's primary responsibility is to make choices that balance the needs of all relevant parties. Organizational politics may be a source of both problems and solutions; effective executives understand this and work to strike a balance between competing interests as they advance the company's strategic objectives. This necessitates adeptly negotiating power relations, encouraging stakeholder collaboration, and making choices that benefit the organization as a whole rather than individual members or special interests.

Symbolic (Act)

Togetherness. Leaders are encouraged to embrace the relevance of symbols and culture within this framework, which promotes Togetherness. Symbols, rituals, and narrative may help them achieve this goal by shaping the organization's identity and inspiring a shared vision. Through the strategic use of symbols, leaders have the power to motivate and inspire their staff, resulting in a shared vision and purpose.

4 Ways to Show
Reverence

Squared Away Leadership Theory

Clarity in Roles

Clarity in a structure is crucial for effective functioning, as it ensures everyone understands their roles and goals. Integrity aligns the structure with core values, fostering trust and a respectful environment. It ensures efficient, ethical systems reflecting the organization's vision and mission, while deep respect for duties and responsibilities is valued.

Optimize Efficiency

Empathy in Design is a principle that emphasizes creating and maintaining structures that are clear, effective, and considerate of the people within them. It involves leaders applying Authentic Empathy to ensure the framework is efficient, supportive, and responsive to team members' needs and well-being.

Alignment with Goals

Make sure the formal structure is a strategic instrument that supports and develops the organization's purpose and vision by linking it with overall objectives; this will emphasize reverence. Strategic organizational design, employee engagement and development, and mission-driven leadership are a few examples.

Respect Stability

Show reverence for the structural frame's efforts to create order and stability by appreciating the need of a clear structure as a building block for success. Investment in one's own professional growth and education are a few examples, as are strict adherence to established corporate protocols and rules.

4 Ways to Show
Intentionality

Personalized Development Plans

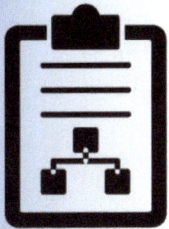

Know that your past and personal story have an effect on how you see the world. Figure out how these things affect how people see things. Being aware of this lets you connect with your true self more consciously. Self-reflection and writing in a diary are two examples. So are culture study and experience and careful listening.

Regular Feedback and Coaching

Take the time to think about your situations and beliefs. Try to figure out how they affect your choices and behaviors. This intentional journey helps you get in touch with your true self and life's meaning. Some examples are doing activities to clarify your ideals, becoming more self-aware, and thinking to find trends.

Empowerment and Autonomy

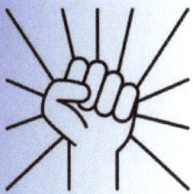

Try to make sure that your behaviors are in line with who you really are. Connect your ideals and views with the things you do every day by using purposeful direction. A better feeling of purpose and authenticity grows from this connection. Setting short- & long-term true goals that are in line with your ideals and making daily practices are two examples.

Investment in Learning Opportunities

Take the time to think about your own thoughts and experiences. Regularly thinking about yourself can help you see and understand the things that shape your view of the world. This leads to a life that is aligned with meaning and authenticity. Mindfulness meditation is a way to think critically about your beliefs and test them.

4 Ways to Show Objectivity

Balanced Decision-Making

Make sure that choices account for overall objectives of the business and take into account the various interests of stakeholders, without showing any prejudice or favoritism. Diversity & inclusion training, conducting stakeholder analyses to guarantee a varied decision-making process, and maintaining open lines of contact with everyone.

Navigating Power Dynamics

Objectivity involves handling these relationships carefully, avoiding excessive influence, and making choices that serve the organization's larger goals rather than giving in to personal or factional demands. Making decisions as a team that includes people from all backgrounds, creating transparent & equitable processes, and leading with integrity and holding people to account are all good examples.

Transparent Communication

In order to promote understanding and reduce misinterpretations, it is important to keep communication lines open and explain choices and their reasoning. Some examples include holding meetings at regular intervals to explain decisions and offer updates, and having a centralized repository for all relevant papers, policies, and resources.

Promoting Cooperation

Encourage open dialogue & teamwork among all parties involved to actively promote cooperation. This dispassionate method reduces the likelihood of disagreements stemming from divergent viewpoints and promotes the development of agreement. Find solutions that work for everyone, try holding collaborative workshops & promoting open communication.

Squared Away Leadership Theory

4 Ways to Show
Togetherness

Symbolic Leadership Actions

Embrace symbolic actions that demonstrate common principles and solidarity. This might take the form of rituals, gatherings, or even visual cues that foster a feeling of Togetherness within the team.

Cultivate Rituals and Traditions

The group should develop and maintain its own set of cultural rites and customs. Continuity is created via these common behaviors, which fosters Togetherness by linking people to a communal identity. Recognizance ceremonies and frequent team-building getaways are two examples.

Strategic Storytelling

An effective way to convey the organization's past, present, & future is the use of stories. To strengthen the team's feeling of Togetherness, it's helpful to create & share tales that everyone can relate to. Highlighting the achievements of people who exemplify the organization's principles & make valuable contributions to its objectives. Formulating & disseminating the organization's ambitions for the future.

Inclusive Decision-Making

Involvement in decision-making processes fosters Togetherness by giving workers a voice in shaping the company's identity and giving them a stake in its future. Among them, you may find task force committees made up of workers from various departments and levels of the company, as well as frequent surveys and feedback channels for employees.

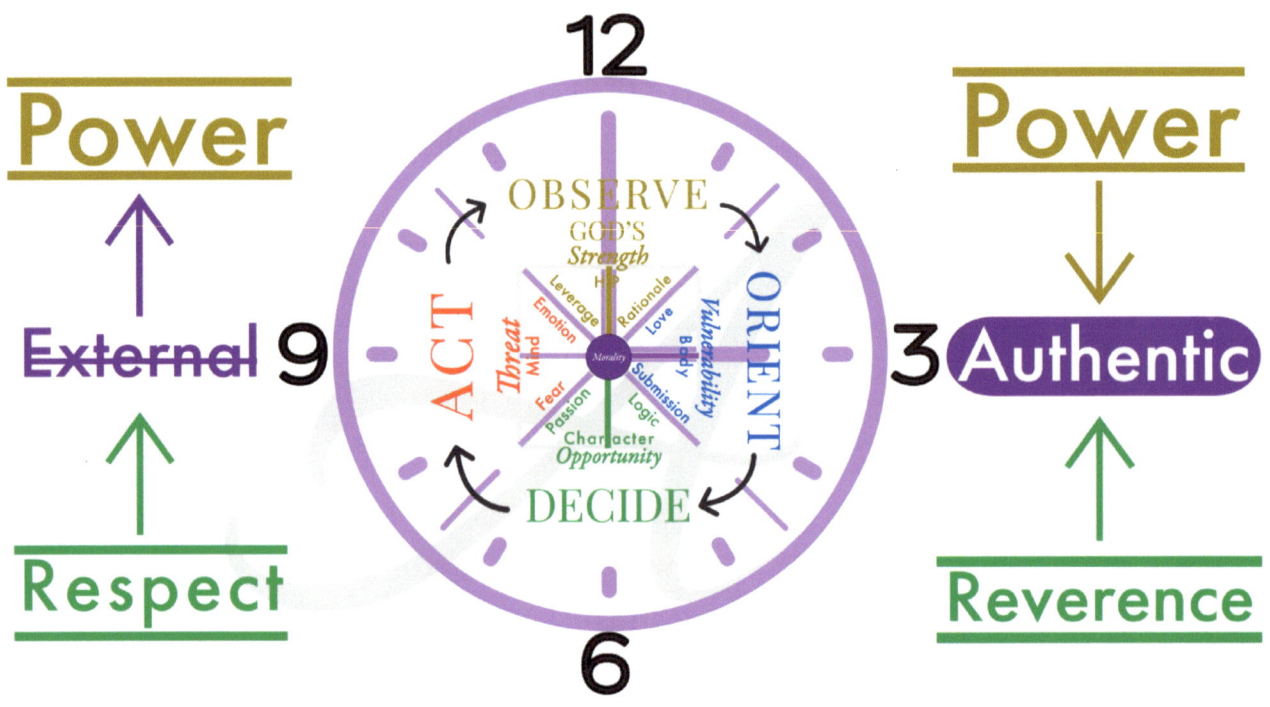

Squared Away
Love Theory

Human

Understanding that love is a natural part of being human is a part of this frame that supports **Reverence**. This point of view goes into detail about how our habits and actions affect how we show and feel love. Emotions are very important to this process because they make us care about others and are the basis of love. But logic also comes into play because the things we do and choose to affect the people we interact with. We can develop reverence for the important part that love plays in our lives and relationships by understanding this interaction between feelings and logic.

Friend

Intentionality is something that this frame aims to foster in the friend frame of love. When it comes to relationships, people should put thought first. From this point of view, love is like a close friendship that is based on shared values, hobbies, and smart, well-thought-out decisions. People who want to live up to this frame should work on building strong logical foundations in their relationships, which is thought to be necessary for making bonds that last and mean something.

Partner

Logic helps us find a reasonable way to move forward, and desire keeps us dedicated to that goal. This frame focuses on **Objectivity** where it's important to connect love with a sense of worth. This method uses both reason and emotion to make love stronger and last longer in relationships. When we focus on shared goals and a sense of purpose, love becomes a driving force that pushes us to reach important goals together. This keeps our relationship objective.

Lover

This frame highlights **Togetherness** by putting the strong emotional bond between lovers first and taking care of it. Passion, which comes from this strong emotional connection, is what makes this kind of love unique. Accept your feelings and let them out in the open; they are what make love so strong. With this emotional link, you can inspire and push each other to face obstacles, be there for each other through good times and bad, and build a love that lasts.

4 Ways to Show
Reverence

Squared Away
Love Theory

Mindful Decision-Making in Relationships

Encourage people to make decisions in relationships with care, understanding that logical choices can change the way love works. To cultivate a sense of reverence for the intentional growth of love, this requires an understanding of how our choices affect the course of our relationships. Some examples are making goals together, resolving conflicts in a thoughtful way, & communicating in a way that makes you think.

Emotional Awareness & Expression

To acknowledge and value the important role emotions play in our lives, especially when it comes to love, encourage people to be emotionally aware and express themselves. Some examples are supporting honest and open conversation, building empathy to understand and accept other people's feelings, and using mindfulness methods to become more emotionally aware.

Promoting Empathy & Understanding

Recognizing the different ways people feel and show love can help build respect & understanding. A feeling of reverence for the depth and variety of human relationships can be developed by acknowledging the differences in each person's emotional environment. Cultural literacy & awareness, communicating with empathy, and respecting personal values and choices are some examples.

Encouraging a Love-Centric Culture

Make a society that values and prioritizes real relationships between people and puts love at its center. This means encouraging actions & habits that show a deep understanding of how important love is in forming our lives and relationships. Promoting open communication, praising diversity & inclusion, and encouraging acts of kindness & support are some examples.

4 Ways to Show
Intentionality

Collective Goal Setting

Show informed togetherness by getting everyone involved in setting and describing group goals. This will help people feel like they have a common cause and are committed to reaching those goals. Some examples are meetings where people work together to set goals, regular check-ins as a team, and activities where everyone shares a vision and set of principles.

Recognition of Individual Contributions

Encourage informed togetherness by recognizing and appreciating the unique things that each person brings to the group. This will help create a culture that values the variety of skills and strengths that each person brings to the group effort. Diverse team-building, making decisions together, and jobs and tasks based on skills are some examples.

Thoughtful Decision-Making

Think carefully about the choices you make about relationships. When making decisions and acting, think about how they will affect you in the long run. When making and keeping links, be thoughtful and intentional. Some examples are figuring out someone's values & fit, learning how to communicate and solve conflicts, and making plans and setting goals.

Shared Values & Interests

Focus on building ties based on shared hobbies and beliefs. Find people whose views and interests are similar to yours on purpose. This will give you a solid foundation for a deep bond. Some examples are joining groups with people who share your interests, using social media to find people who share your values, and working for issues you care about.

4 Ways to Show Objectivity

Goal Alignment Discussions

Talk with each other to figure out what goals and aims you both want to achieve in the relationship. This method makes sure that choices and actions are based on a group goal instead of individual wants. Checking in on a relationship daily, working together to find common ground, & writing down a relationship mission statement are all examples.

Balancing Rationality & Emotion

Take your logic and emotions into account when you're talking and making decisions. Know how important it is to use logic, but let emotion and determination drive the pursuit of common goals. Emotional intelligence training, frameworks for making decisions that take both logical and emotional factors into account, and positive conversation are some examples.

Communication Grounded in Purpose

Make sure that the relationship's conversation is centered on the shared goals & purpose. This helps people stay objective by keeping the conversation on how activities fit into the bigger picture. For example, before having important talks, people should be encouraged to explain how their efforts fit into the bigger picture. There should also be clear rules for how to communicate.

Regular Review of Shared Objectives

Review and reevaluate the relationship's shared goals on a regular basis. This makes it possible to objectively check if the actions and efforts are in line with the goal that everyone agreed upon. Check-ins to go over shared goals daily, goal-setting and visioning events, and feedback and review sessions are all examples.

4 Ways to Show
Togetherness

Unwavering Support in Challenges

Being there for your partner through hard times is very important. To reinforce the idea that Togetherness is a source of strength, this may entail actively listening, encouraging, & working through difficulties as a team. Some examples are active listening & understanding with empathy, positive feedback and support, and making decisions and fixing problems together.

Open Expressions of Emotions

It's important to talk about feelings in an open and honest way. Openly talking about your feelings, wants, and weaknesses can help your relationship grow emotionally. Setting up a safe space where no one will judge you, doing regular emotional check-ins, and using "I statements" to talk about your own feelings and experiences instead of blaming your partner are all examples.

Mutual Motivation & Inspiration

Use your strong emotional connection to spur each other on. To build a feeling of shared purpose and Togetherness, help each other reach their goals, support each other's personal growth, and enjoy each other's successes. Sharing goals, giving and receiving helpful comments and support, and personal growth programs are some examples.

Building Enduring Love

Put your attention on building a love that will last. Spend time and energy building the emotional link. This will lay the groundwork for a strong and long-lasting love bond that grows stronger over time. Some examples are talking to each other regularly and in a useful way, having shared experiences and valuable time, and being able to change & grow together.

Map of Consciousness

Developed By David R. Hawkins

	Name of Level	Energetic Log	Predominant Emotional State	View of Life	God-view	Process
Spiritual Paradigm	Enlightenment	700-1000	Ineffable	Is	Self	Pure Consciousness
	Peace	600	Bliss	Perfect	All-Being	Illumination
	Joy	540	Serenity	Complete	One	Transfiguration
	Love	500	Reverence	Benign	Loving	Revelation
Reason & Integrity	Reason	400	Understanding	Meaningful	Wise	Abstraction
	Acceptance	350	Forgiveness	Harmonious	Merciful	Transcendence
	Willingness	310	Optimism	Hopeful	Inspiring	Intention
	Neutrality	250	Trust	Satisfactory	Enabling	Release
	Courage	200	Affirmation	Feasible	Permitting	Empowerment
Survival Paradigm	Pride	175	Scorn	Demanding	Indifferent	Inflation
	Anger	150	Hate	Antagonistic	Vengeful	Aggression
	Desire	125	Craving	Disappointing	Denying	Enslavement
	Fear	100	Anxiety	Frightening	Punitive	Withdrawal
	Grief	75	Regret	Tragic	Disdainful	Despondency
	Apathy	50	Despair	Hopeless	Condemning	Abdication
	Guilt	30	Blame	Evil	Vindictive	Destruction
	Shame	20	Humiliation	Miserable	Despising	Elimination

Source credit: https://life-longlearner.com/how-to-measure-consciousness-using-the-map-of-consciousness-3-of-7/

References / Reading List

- "The Seat of the Soul" by Gary Zukav
- "The 48 Laws of Power" by Robert Greene
- "Thinking Fast and Slow" by Daniel Kahneman
- "Lies My teacher Told Me" by James Loewen
- "The Art of Seduction" by Robert Greene
- "Unf*ck Yourself" by Gary John Bishop
- "Switch: How to Change Things When Change Is Hard" by Heath Brothers
- "The Five Love Languages" by Dr. Gary Chapman
- "The Five Appreciation Languages" by Dr. Gary Chapman and Dr. Paul White
- "The Righteous Mind: Why Good People are Divided by Politics and Religion" by Jonathan Haidt
- "Reframing Organizations: Artistry, Choice, and Leadership" by Lee G. Bolman and Terrence E. Deal
- "Never Split the Difference: Negotiating As If Your Life Depended On It" by Chris Voss and Tahl Rax
- "Transitions" by William Bridges
- "The Alchemist" by Paulo Coelho
- "Made To Stick: Why Some Ideas Survive and Others Die" by Heath Brothers
- "Talking To Strangers: What We Should Know About the People We Don't Know" by Malcolm Gladwell
- "Essentialism: The Disciplined Pursuit of Less" by Greg McKeown
- "The Fifth Discipline: The Art & Practice of The Learning Organization" by Peter M. Senge
- "Friends: Understanding the Power of Our Most Important Relationships" by Robin Dunbar
- "White Frugility: Why It's Hard for White People to Talk About Racism" by Dr. Robin DiAngelo and Michael Eric Dyson
- "White Trash: The 400-Year Untold History of Class in America" by Nancy Isenberg, Kristen Potter, et al.
- "The Souls of Black Folks" by W.E.B. Du Bois
- "How to Attract Money" by Joseph Murphy
- "Black Privilege: Opportunity Comes to Those Who Create It" by Charlamagne Tha God
- "Between the World and Me" by Ta-Neihisi Coates
- "Naked Statistics" by Charles Wheelan
- "Think With Intention" by Peter Hollins
- "You vs. You" by Michael J Stevens
- "Overstanding" by Kalvin R. Johnson, The Reporter | Volume 43, Number 4

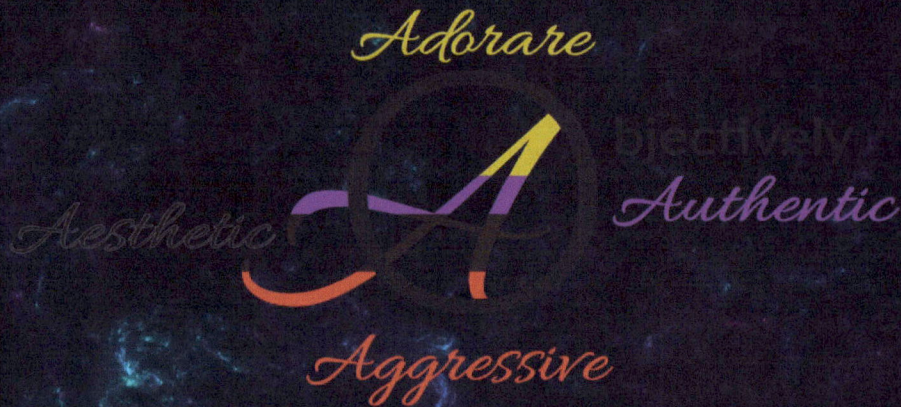

The Squared Away Leadership Theory (SALT) is the foundation of **Objectively Aesthetic** (OA), emphasizing Structural (**Reverence**), Human Resources (**Intentionality**), Political (**Objectivity**), and Symbolic (**Togetherness** frameworks.

Objectively Adorare promotes Reverence through its clothing line, encouraging spiritual and aesthetic appreciation.

Objectively Authentic focuses on Intentionality by fostering genuine connections and meaningful content.

Objectively Aggressive applies the Political framework with balanced content in its PodKast series, navigating diverse interests.

Objectively Aesthetic uses the Symbolic framework, integrating various professional vocations to present beauty and unity.

Together, these elements uphold OA's mission to promote light & love energy through **Reverence**, **Intentionality**, **Objectivity**, and **Togetherness**.

VISION  MISSION

VISION

To overstand vision & voice to excel in all frameworks of society. To find reverence in business and in life to provide a cultural competence experience.

MISSION

To encourage individuals to seek a clear path to authenticity & purpose. To provide an understanding of cultural IQ & organizational leadership resulting in global & noble possibilities.

CORE VALUES

R

Reverence

With a deep respect for perspective, diversity, innovation, and tradition, we approach every challenge with humility and understanding. Reverence is providing and fostering an environment of Inclusion that welcomes Early Adopters with Binocular vision to collaboratively envision and shape innovative solutions and initiatives.

I

Intentionality

We work closely with our clients to help them define their perspectives and goals, clarify their vision, and develop strategic plans that are both purposeful and actionable. We believe that every decision, every strategy, and every action should be driven by a clear sense of purpose.

O

Objectivity

We understand that unbiased, data-driven insights are the foundation of effective decision-making and problem-solving. We are committed to providing clients with clear, impartial, and evidence-based recommendations, free from personal biases or hidden agendas.

T

Togetherness

This core value is rooted in the understanding that when individuals unite their skills, knowledge, and perspectives, they can achieve remarkable results. We are committed to helping organizations harness the power of unity to drive growth, innovation, and lasting success.

Added Bonus!

Kalvin R. Johnson's "OVERstanding: The Paralegal Instructor Perspective" from The Reporter |Volume 43, Number 4

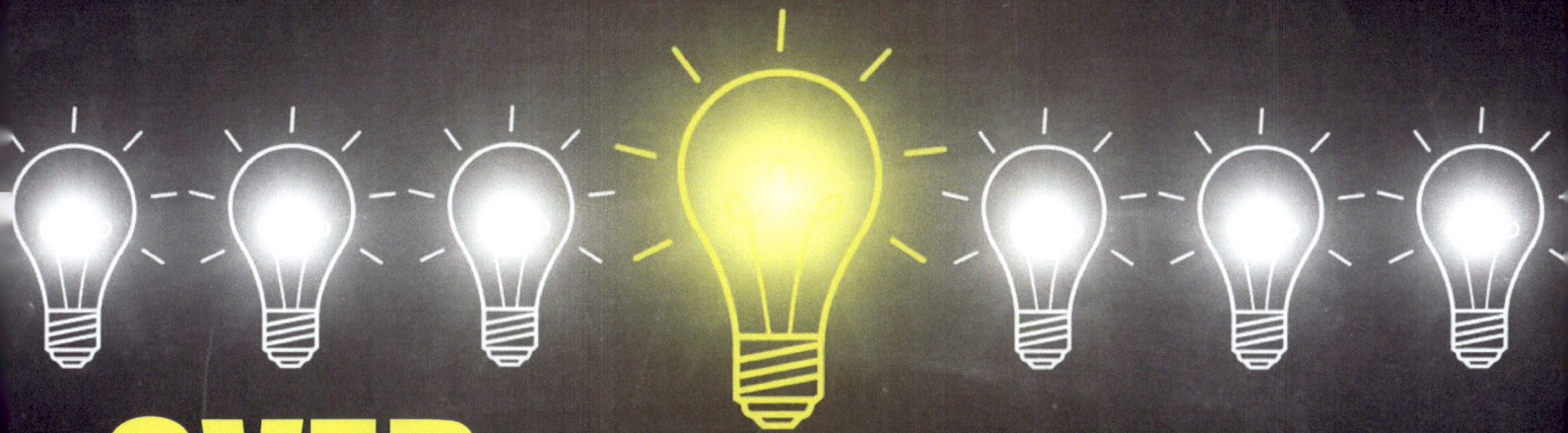

OVERSTANDING
The Paralegal Instructor Perspective

BY TECHNICAL SERGEANT KALVIN R. JOHNSON

> To have long term success as a coach or in any position of leadership, you have to obsess in some way.

As a student in the Paralegal Craftsman's Course (PCC or 7-Level), I watched how my instructors presented the curriculum and I looked at them with a smirk on my face as if to say: "Instructing is too easy." Not particularly impressed by the instruction, and sometimes bored with the presentation, I would find myself daydreaming or even discussing the possibility of becoming a paralegal instructor myself. After all, from where I sat, it seemed like anyone could excel at the job. At times my cavalier attitude irritated the instructor staff. So I'm sure you can imagine how awkward it was when I showed up less than 3 months later and was greeted by those same instructors, who were now my peers and co-workers. I was quickly humbled by the monumental challenges of being a paralegal instructor at The Judge Advocate General's School

(JAG School) and eventually had to apologize to my fellow instructors for my hubris. In the end, however, I mastered the skills I needed to instruct. How did I do it? I'm glad you asked!

As a paralegal instructor at the JAG School my primary goal is to turn United States Air Force Airmen into legal professionals. A legal professional is one who studies, develops, and applies the law. Becoming a legal professional, whether a lawyer or a paralegal, requires special training. My fellow instructors and I have the unique opportunity to provide that training to a diverse population of students, varying in age (18–50), experience, service (active duty, guard, and reserve), and education level. There is immense pressure on instructors to educate a diverse student body which could contain a student straight out of high school sitting right next to a student who has already completed or is in the process of completing law school in their civilian capacity. Pat Riley once said, "To have long term success as a coach or in any position of leadership, you have to obsess in some way."[1] I remind myself of this quote every time I prepare to teach the diverse group of students who flow through the JAG School. I embrace the obsession that I feel is required to be a competent instructor by implementing what I call "overstanding."

OVERSTANDING VS UNDERSTANDING

Overstanding is my way of describing the level of knowledge and preparation one must possess to lead a class of paralegal students, and—for that matter—to be a leader in general. Leaders must understand their subject and situation in a way that allows them to think on their feet, analyze the situation, and then respond quickly and accurately. Overstanding is a level of knowledge above understanding. It involves incorporating the different types of learning to create a dynamic learning environment. How can I teach or lead if I only "understand" the subject I'm expected to teach? Students taking the class want to understand to pass the test; I need to overstand to produce the type of inspired teaching that will help them pass the test *and* learn the skills

[1] Pat Riley Quotes, BRAINYQUOTE.COM, http://www.brainyquote.com/quotes/quotes/p/patriley147937.html (last visited 11 September 2016).

they need to effectively accomplish their mission as legal professionals. Instructors must be subject matter experts in estate planning, civil law, and criminal law to teach students competently. The common saying in the JAG Corps is: "JA stands for 'just ask.'" This quote implies that everyone asks legal professionals questions about anything you can imagine.

Students taking the class want to understand to pass the test; I need to overstand to produce the type of inspired teaching that will help them pass the test and learn the skills they need to effectively accomplish their mission as legal professionals.

But who do legal professionals ask? The students at JAG School expect their instructors to be competent and diligent. We are mentors, leaders, and wingmen. Students, mentees, subordinates, and superiors all want answers and results, which is why the concept of overstanding is so important. The training to become a paralegal instructor goes a long way to helping would-be instructors to begin to overstand.

INSTRUCTOR TRAINING

The first step to become a paralegal instructor is completion of the 5-week Basic Instructor Course. Then new instructors complete an internship in which they must achieve a minimum of 120 contact hours of supervised instruction with students. These contact hours include teaching under the supervision of an experienced and fully qualified instructor; classroom management; and integrating technology into various phases of the curriculum. While going through the internship, the new instructor is called a "student instructor." Student instructors "backseat" the Paralegal Apprentice Courses (PAC or 3-Level). The process is called "back seating," because the student instructors sit in the back of a classroom and observe a qualified instructor teach the class. Shortly after "back seating," the student instructor is then required to teach PAC, twice before being a certified Subject Matter Expert Instructor. I coined it "the 16 weeks of stress." It is an especially difficult time filled with long days of instruction, grading, mentoring, and then long nights of preparing to do it all over again. I realized during that part of my training that this career path was not for the faint of heart.

Once an instructor has completed his or her internship, and demonstrated proficiency as an instructor in the classroom, a wide array of teaching, curriculum development, and leadership opportunities become available. Active duty, reservists, and guardsmen come to the JAG School for both initial skills training in the PAC and upgrade training in the Paralegal Craftsman Course (PCC or 7-Level). Most paralegal instructors work in the Paralegal Development Division (PDD), which is responsible for teaching PAC PCC, and Serving as course directors for in-residence courses as well as Distance Learning courses. Paralegal instructors can also transition into the Military Training Leader (MTL) position. MTLs focus on enforcing military training and standards that support the newly enlisted Airmen's continued transition into military life. The MTL and paralegal instructors have the opportunity to educate commissioned officers as well. From uniform inspections to teaching Military Justice and Adverse Actions, paralegal instructors have a direct effect on personnel development. Paralegal instructors also have an opportunity to work outside of PDD and transition to the Accreditation, Curriculum and Evaluation (ACE) Division. This role requires an evaluation of course curriculum and Paralegal Instructor development and training. ACE is tasked with the responsibility of making sure the paralegal program meets the Community College of the Air Force (CCAF) requirements and remains certified by the American Bar Association (ABA). Being well rounded is just one of the attributes required to perform. Paralegal instructors also have direct effects on the operation of the JAG School and the operational Air Force. Instructors train students that go directly into the workforce using their acquired knowledge and skills.

BEYOND INSTRUCTING

Another part of being an Air Force instructor is the requirement to demonstrate impeccable adherence to Air Force customs and courtesies, dress and appearance, and core values. For this reason, I like to think of Air Force instructors as "culture pilots." We are expected to epitomize these areas of the Air Force profession of arms and rely on them when mentoring our students. As non-commissioned officers (NCOs), we lead subordinates toward a deeper understanding of self-discipline and adherence to the high standards of the Air Force, but we also advise and support our superiors to facilitate efficient mission accomplishment. As instructors, we are expected to know everything about how to wear the uniform properly, to how to conduct an advisement of Article 31 rights, and the meaning and implications of the Fourth, Fifth and Sixth Amendments. How can one lead in any area when they are not versed on the topic? Successful instructor leaders cannot afford to merely understand; they must overstand. Overstanding requires an obsession with success. You must think and function at a higher level in anticipation of what may come. Overstanding benefits the individual as well as the team. If the leader clearly overstands the issues at hand, the leader can effectively communicate the path to a solution. When we overstand each other, we can overtake any obstacle.

Overstanding is also a professional gift to superiors.

CONCLUSION

To say being an instructor is demanding is an understatement. The concept of overstanding is paramount to the overall success of an instructor in any environment. When it comes to teaching at the JAG School, I learned that it takes diligence and commitment to walk into a classroom ready to teach the finest Airmen in the Air Force to be legal professionals. It takes character and confidence to embody the highest standards of leadership and to embrace the role of "culture pilots" for both the newest Airmen and the seasoned NCOs. Using overstanding as a vehicle has allowed me to relish the challenging and ever-changing world of being an JAG School paralegal instructor. And now I can truly say the rewards are well worth the endeavor. [R]

**Technical Sergeant
Kalvin R. Johnson**

(A.S., Community College of the Air Force) recently PCS'd from the JAG School to become the Noncommissioned Officer in Charge of Adverse Actions, 96th Test Wing, Eglin Air Force Base, Florida.

www.ingramcontent.com/pod-product-compliance
Lightning Source LLC
Chambersburg PA
CBHW041544260326
41914CB00015B/1547